A Crabtree Roots Book

FARM ANIMAL FRIENDS
TURKEYS

AMY CULLIFORD

CRABTREE
Publishing Company
www.crabtreebooks.com

School-to-Home Support for Caregivers and Teachers

This book helps children grow by letting them practice reading. Here are a few guiding questions to help the reader with building his or her comprehension skills. Possible answers appear here in red.

Before Reading:

- What do I think this book is about?
    - *I think this book is about turkeys.*
    - *I think this book is about turkeys and their friends on the farm.*
- What do I want to learn about this topic?
    - *I want to learn what turkeys eat.*
    - *I want to learn if turkeys can fly.*

During Reading:

- I wonder why...
    - *I wonder why turkeys come in so many different colors.*
    - *I wonder why some turkeys say gobble.*
- What have I learned so far?
    - *I have learned that all turkeys have feathers.*
    - *I have learned that all turkeys have beaks.*

After Reading:

- What details did I learn about this topic?
    - *I have learned that some turkeys are big, and some are little.*
    - *I have learned that turkeys usually live on a farm.*
- Read the book again and look for the vocabulary words.
    - *I see the word **feathers** on page 8, and the word **beaks** on page 10. The other vocabulary words are found on page 14.*

This is a **turkey**.

Some turkeys are big, and some are little.

Turkeys can be brown, black, or white.

All turkeys have **feathers**.

All turkeys have **beaks**.

Some turkeys say, *gobble*!

Word List

Sight Words

a	black	or
all	brown	say
and	can	some
are	have	this
be	is	white
big	little	

Words to Know

beaks

feathers

turkey

31 Words

This is a **turkey**.

Some turkeys are big, and some are little.

Turkeys can be brown, black, or white.

All turkeys have **feathers**.

All turkeys have **beaks**.

Some turkeys say, *gobble*!

FARM ANIMAL FRIENDS
TURKEYS

CRABTREE Publishing Company

Written by: Amy Culliford
Designed by: Rhea Wallace
Series Development: James Earley
Proofreader: Petrice Custance
Educational Consultant: Christina Lemke M.Ed.

Photographs:
Shutterstock: Jennay Hitesman: cover (top left); Alexey Sauchuk: cover (top right); Unkas Photo: (cover bottom); Kingcraft: p. 1; Oguz Dikbakan; p. 3; Natallia Ustsinava: p. 5; mnapoli: p. 6-7; Bearok: p. 9; Casey Dugas: p. 11; Tom Reichner: p. 12

Library and Archives Canada Cataloguing in Publication

CIP available at Library and Archives Canada

Library of Congress Cataloging-in-Publication Data

CIP available at Library of Congress

Crabtree Publishing Company

www.crabtreebooks.com 1-800-387-7650

 Printed in the U.S.A./072022/CG20220201

 In Canada: We acknowledge the financial support of the Government of Canada through the Canada Book Fund for our publishing activities.

Published in the United States
Crabtree Publishing
347 Fifth Avenue, Suite 1402-145
New York, NY, 10016

Published in Canada
Crabtree Publishing
616 Welland Ave.
St. Catharines, ON, L2M 5V6